WITHDRAWN

D1075116

MOSTLY PEOPLE

JEANNETTE NICHOLS

RUTGERS UNIVERSITY PRESS

NEW BRUNSWICK, NEW JERSEY

Grateful acknowledgment is made to the following publications for permission to reprint poems which originally appeared in them:

The American Scholar: Three Flights Up in Rome.

Antioch Review: Fish Man; Hear; Mirror; Woman of Brown Skin.

The Atlantic Monthly: Bliss Sleeps; Dike Diving; Fast Run in the Junkyard; Girl in a Green Dress; Loping West at Twenty-one; My Father Toured the South; My Half of the Apple; One Day; One Thing Leads to Another and; The Same Lady.

The Beloit Poetry Journal: A Peacock, Black Swan and Now These Gulls.

The Carleton Miscellany: Someone Gone Away Downstairs.

Carolina Quarterly: A Kind of Love; Figurine.

Harper's Magazine, Inc.: The Return.

Magazine of Fantasy and Science Fiction: The Light and the Sadness.

Mutiny: Asylum Fire.

Prairie Schooner: Horses of Stone; Lady of Honors; Picasso.

Quarterly Review of Literature: Promise to an Unconceived Child.

Saturday Review: Any Time, Any Place; Artist as Rhinoceros; Blackberries; Found: A Slip of Almost White Paper; Ivory Tower; Kingdoms; Kneeling by the Window; A Man I Know; Mostly People; Much Too Sane; No One Here But Us; Once We Ate Roses; To Rico Lebrun and Anger at Buchenwald; Truth Has a Singing; What Got Away; Wonder's Shoes; A Zest, an Ache, an Itch.

The Southern Review: The Question.

Yale Literary Magazine: Simultaneous Inch, Two Reasons for the Phantom Child.

To
Dick Banks
[*for us all*]
and
Shaosh
[*for myself*]

CONTENTS

A PEACOCK, BLACK SWAN
AND NOW THESE GULLS

I see again Catalina,
see one white peacock beneath a wire dome,
and one black swan like a lord
going round and round a lonely castle;
see the dirt road
with a single eucalyptus
canted on the hillside
and myself walking
that far-gone west-coast
way-off island road,
on my way to nothing but birds.
From this citadel of ten-years gone,
I stand stoned by a peculiar beauty
caught in my youth
as I watch gutter-dirty gulls lusting
it over this other ocean;
and on my way back from the past
I find more beauty
in their short dog-barks,
larking the air for free food
and a hutch of wind,
than in that remembered peacock
walking the rounds of a wire world
and the strange black swan
caught in his own dark ripples.

DIKE DIVING

I never dived the Dike,
remembering a sea-bagged body
caught in its floating hinge;
but walked it watching
the loud brave bodies sound
the seaweed where
the dug channel churned
like the boil of an unmade mind,
watched and waited
for the ones who didn't come up
dead and smashed like eels
the fishermen dashed against
the Dike walls. I dreamed leaning
above the curliqued water, dreamed
of going down lead-weight straight,
down where hairy seaweed dressed me
and eels pressed close for curiosity,
dreamed myself half saved
from the Dike doors and tugging tides.
And the sun was greater and better
than food when I'd straighten up alive
to the arcs of netted fish, spray raining
up from the diving, and sea winds
looser than water to breathe, balancing
along the Dike again,
feeling the dare float off
like candy wrappers down the channel.

BLACKBERRIES

We hunted blackberries
in the ruins of the old Highland Hotel
salt-seasoned on its bluff
where they lurked, fat and black
bees eyes in the secret deeps
of the rubble. Half the first floor
hung like sprung bridgework, the stairs
tunneling down like a throat
to where the brambles dipped
and boiled live with fruit.
Double-dared we clutched
our bags like empty lungs
inching down to where the chalk-dark
dried our breath and Summer shriveled
thin as the hairs of light the boards let in;
but climbed back up
with mouths, teeth and tongues
gloriously horrible
and paper-stained bags
sagging with black loot.

A ZEST, AN ACHE, AN ITCH

I've gone out before,
been riled at the streets,
stores, tailored mailboxes,
and roared off in full horsepower
to burn back roads, byways, rutted
dirt lanes with their hangdog trees,
and even then not eased it. I've
boasted along blocks
looking in at dinners, readers,
pedigreed winners of their daily
dog-tired bread
and found no salve to soothe it.
I've let it nab me
like an itch,
stitch me like an ache,
squeeze my love-gland dry;
and been bested by it
in the fast and far coast towns
where I've tried to run it down.
It has flashed like summer lightning
by me in the bashed, down-trodden faces
dashing at better-times,
bared its hook-nose,
sick-limb, lame-eye, truth and lie
in this slick and human town
I collide with;

but it's still there
to chase and tame me
till I go after it again
on the hopped train, next plane
out, full of the healthy rage
to rout the lust that drives me
crack-brained, full-tilt,
head-on through.

MY FATHER TOURED
THE SOUTH

My father and his muscles
toured the South posing
in store windows stripped down
past his biceps. He was young then,
dark eyes like dates, hair
like a black sandbar. Full of rush
to crush cities and worlds
like the air he shushed off
when he brought the loose strap up
round his chest and inhaled
till he filled it, proving
the power of physical culture.

When I was nine and he in the forties
I found his pictures, profiled in tights
like a small John L. He laughed
when I showed them, and with a thumb
in his mouth blew up his arm
like an auto tire we tried
to squeeze down and couldn't.

Now that proud and laughing strength
folds to a memory of store windows
and caught ohs from his children's lips
as he hefted us up to the ceiling
and swung us back like easy dumbbells.
His arms are half-caste traitors to a wish
with no more weights to lift,

nothing his youth need move by muscle,
no cities to push flat for the sake
of proving strength. Only the muscles in his head
still flex and dance as his arms did once
in that old thumb game and the strap
across his brain pulls tight again and again.

FAST RUN

IN THE JUNKYARD

That junkyard fell down the side of the hill
like a river: baby buggy, black leather
cracked car back seat, sofa wind-siphoned
by a clutch of tangled wire hangers hanging on
like spiders. We stood and fell as momentum told us
toward somebody's sodden Sealy dying of galloping
   miasma,
jumped on bedsprings sprung to pogos, and leaped
for king-of-the-mountain where boxes and cans
   fountained
up the hill's other side. Sailing saucers, we rode
back down, flinging hat racks, burlap sacks, chairs
   cropped
of backs and flotsam crockery, breezed in league boots
back out of everybody's past hazards, up to the road
to break tar bubbles all-the-way-home where things
were wearing out as fast as we were growing up.

THE ABSOLUTE OF RUNNING

The absolute of running
like every perfection
breaks and rebreaks. Surely
as dedicated as limbs in prayer,
convinced only that the ground goes
under a kind of uncanny
mechanics, one hastened stride
is cog for the next. Oiled
by a spaced breathing
the wheel of running turns,
absolute and rooted only by push
and touch, leaving and coming
propelled to somewhere other,
somewhere fast, somewhere breathless,
somewhere absolutely nowhere else.

LOPING WEST

AT TWENTY-ONE

Greyhound and four and a half days
to get to L.A. What we had to say of
so-long was said and we were off at twenty-one,

hardly done with ruling notebooks,
but off to (speak softly) California.
We learned a form of greyhound sleep

at knees and heels with night, you
too tall for ease, and all short snores
teasing my slumber. But we went

greyhound swimming through four nights
of rolling west and lived for the dark
coffee stops and lopping miles.

Went to California in a hush to live
and match our memories
between those bookend seas

that held our worlds apart. You planted
what you had of heart in that Pacific
dust and I hiked my lust home East

to learn the least things overlooked
in this New England town I took
for dull and lagging every-day;

and later watched the greyhounds lope west
again remembering the year we were twenty-one
(was it only one?) running to catch life.

ONE DAY

One day
like no other
Vermont
undefined in early mists
into which we woke
in a tent
my Father and I
and moved in our damp bones
around woodsmoke
while the mists burned away
and three crows flew over
knowing everything;

one morning like no other
my Father with eyes full of woodsmoke and tears
and I
trampling Vermont's indistinct wet grass
saw those crows fly over
in dry dark shapes,
felt three
flickering shadows
cross our faces
as quick as love.

DISCOVERING, A PHOTOGRAPH

There is your face,
eyes full of waiting,
small mouth tasting a smile

you are my friend

and you are nineteen yet to be married
or loved in the secret reaches
of Asbury Park, in the dark
and secret beaches
of my father's mind.

But here you are a friend
in my hands, hair haloed back
with a band, a look in your eyes
I've had in mine.

My blind eyes see you.

And somewhere you are sixty-six
as I am thirty-three
the age you were the day you bore me

my mother, my friend, hello

I know you then
and discover you now
hazel-eyed girl looking up from my hands

my mouth tastes the same smile.

FACE IN THE WINDOW

Every day in that house
a face hangs
in the top pane
like a porcelain egg
the same as the one
with violets painted on
we had at home.
And every day
in that window
the egg (which is a face)
looks out
at me
going by
toward everything.
Every day
I speak to the egg
that is something else
(I forget),
speak of how
every one of those violets
is washed off
now.

BLUE

Because someone left
blue tissue paper
on the front steps
I had to write you this letter,
and remembering how
that blue torn kite
caught in the tree bright
and broken as a splash of water
I had to tell you how
this tissue feels
in my hands
as I wash it over one,
over the other.
I had to write
because of the blue
and all broken pasts
and because
my blue hands
won't dry.

FIRST LESSON

Morning glories sucked air,
it was afternoon.
                    I buried the shoebox
with its red dead fur at the foot
of tiger lilies. No marking.
With the raw earth mounded under my hands
I hunkered and watched long shadows
grow longer, listened to tiger lilies slish
against themselves, the sound
certain soft thighs make.
                    All the years of love
lay under my hands, raw earth the color
of raw fur, the color of adolescence.
I was grown before I grew to it,
some of the dead animal eating into me
until, a bending tiger lily
slid along my wrist
as a cat will
loving.

OUT THERE

Out there
is the grown up
world cornered like the box
we kept small importances safe in
long ago when *out there*
was where we went to
when we grew up. And now,
grown up, *out there* is where death
works oiling hinges
while we pace off
between doors
and learn the size
of our boxed-in lives
in here.

NOW, TWO

Dead plain girl, Millicent,
now four years away,
and Peter, you, two months raw gone,
how do I speak of you?

                  My own death
is there
as yours was. Always
we move like arrows.
But to understand?

               Knowing
nothing perfect I live again
that four-year far off Summer
and this one. We were away
from each other and any news
when it came was old.

                You, Millicent,
in your Connecticut bed
embroiled in a last young wardrobe;

              and you, Peter,
fallen and broken like a luckless animal
in a Greece I can only imagine;

you two, four years
and countries apart come home to me
together now
and all I may understand of you,
of myself,
amounts to arrows, arrows.

SOMEONE DYING

[for Aunt Aggie]

Something enters her face,
something named once in sleep
now forgotten as a stranger
is.   She listens
with the look of the deaf who cannot hear
what they have always listened for.
She is.   Dying.

And something enters her eyes
like the bemused smile
of the wise who know
in silence.
She is.   Waiting.

And something enters her arms,
a dearer holding,
a slower letting go.
She knows.   Going.

And something enters my face,
something hers
to take away.
I am.   Dying.
But not now.

ONCE WE ATE ROSES

Once we ate rose petals
rolling pearls of dew and all

bit the bottoms
off honeysuckle buds

chewed mint
but now it's bread

and we
are nearly always hungry.

KINGDOMS

You have come into this personal childhood
as a visitor comes
holding a newly blocked hat
and polite as policemen are sometimes.

Thine is my kingdom if I let you in.

The bushes are low here,
leapable. You are the child I am.
Your hat is useless. Scale it
like a stone on the wind.
                    There
is rushing water we shall walk through,
and here you must leave your shoes.
Those trees are how the other world is:
way off, tall, and we have no time to climb.

Mine is your kingdom if you stay.

ARTIST AS RHINOCEROS

The rhinoceros goes home
to open
    tubes of blue paint
    and be sad.
But without his glasses
he mistakes the labels and squirts
an alizarin snake across a sheet of glass
and sucks in his breath
    suddenly in love.
    All night long
the back of the red snake goes solid
and the rhinoceros
rambling into a terrible dawn
    keeps looking for someone.
    And all night long
the tubes of blue paint
with their loose caps
            wait.

MOSTLY PEOPLE

It's mostly people
who make the world happen.

Steeped with them,
mornings are ridden like buses
and they strap-hang
their wondrous occasional faces
into movies and mealtimes
and lovebeds.
New and small and peculiar
people get born every inhale,
come and gone
like little old men
and little old women
who suck and bawl
and grow up and up
to cram sideways into all
those grand yesterdays
they learn to believe in.

And it's mostly people
who make the others necessary,
like to love, to give to,
to buy from and curse at;
and without such a half-cocked,

people-pocked kind of world
which has locked us all up
in one bright birthday package
to open at any whim of a face,

why then, to be born and get dead
would be just one long yawn.

ONE THING

LEADS TO ANOTHER AND

the chair
so placed requires
a table which consequently requires
an ashtray into which
the next visitor will put
ashes.

The room
somehow requires
a bed which blankly requires
blankets under which
a woman requires
a man to put out
the light
        which is
beside the bed
next to the chair
where the table was placed
just so the ashtray could receive
(before the light went out)
ashes.

SIMULTANEOUS INCH

The simultaneous inch
of love—
whether she speaks it
or he merely rethinks
the mechanical softness
of her innocent animal ways—
is there,
grown upright in air
quietly
as the secretion of trees.

THE RETURN

For a long time now
I have not been able to write you
(the attendants here steal words)
but they have installed new windows,
replaced the door that had the meshed window
near the top (this door opens out)
and I can tell you
how it is
I came here. You remember about
the trees, and the night
the rain came in
took me by both my hands
out (I've never gone back).
After that
I learned to eat nuts, flowers,
sweet shards of wind
caught ripe off the sea (we all survive
as best we can). But the diet
changes, I've learned here
to make lettuce sandwiches, to drink
from melons and peaches (the water is impure)
and I get on. They tell me
you are asking how I am
so I am writing to say
I am, at least I think I am
and (should this new door open out again)

will see you
when you come carrying
the name I once wore
like an almond between your teeth.
You'll know me
by the verb love pinned to my dress
like a fresh Palm Sunday cross.
And if I forget who you are
(my habit is to finger the verb
hoping to remember)
please smile, say who I am
and lead me back,
(all my words are packed)
there's nothing for me here.

WONDER'S SHOES

[for Anne]

Wonder had worn its same shoes
all the many years it lived in your house
and you turned it out barefoot,
said the shoes were done in,
unmendable. It went
as it always goes when told
stubbing its toes on rock.

You vowed to throw all the old things out,
the dolls, broken chair, the lock of hair in the locket.
While Wonder wandered the countryside, child of
    youth,
you cleaned your house, scoured Hope of its skin
before you'd let Wonder back in
to live in its old room,
before you'd wash Wonder's feet
and dry them with new linen,
putting away the first coin toward new shoes.

BLISS SLEEPS

A kind of bliss sleeps
on Bowery street smiling
toward Tuesday and a dish-washing dollar.

Curled, hands tucked into armpits,
sleeping an unworried sleep
bliss dreams

of all the world's white
horses bridled and reined for
the ride home to banners and drums,

home where the bottles are full,
street lights steady and all
the old chances lined up

ready as duck pins.

WOMAN OF BROWN SKIN

Woman of brown skin
                with that kettle head
set waggily above that
                flagstone smile
I wonder
        how my lisping mind
                would wear your darkness.
My fair hands
        are inadequately spaced
                according to your
                smooth rhythmic brown
and my milk thighs
                seem lesser panthers
                       than yours.
But mostly I envy
                your coffee breasts
          that come from your body
                in such volcanic rise.
Yet blood comes into my pasture
                in much the same despair
                    as yours
          and your soft gaze
              confirms our
                similar loss.

FISH MAN

The sound of the fish man's horn
turns the noon sour
as the drips from his ice-packed truck.
Aproned women with coin purses
hurry to stand judging
over the slick catch and haggle
with the bright eyes of the snaggle-toothed
fish man. Small vomits of change
spill as slick as liquid into his thick
hands after he flings each fish
into a flange of paper
handing it over with lips smiling
and eyes deadly enterprising,
eyes as opaque and roomy with death
as the rows of assorted fish
he totes to the next stop.

ANY TIME, ANY PLACE

The fun house mirror
any time, any place,
makes of her face
a Modigliani
meant to be funny
but lovely,
lovely as sadness
bought at a great
price. She moves
closer, goes narrower,
any time, any place,
grows as stark
as a tiger lily.
But someone coming
into the mirror
laughs. She breaks,
and the portrait
goes comic
as she turns
on short legs
any time, any place,
and all that tall
loveliness drains
off like water.

LADY OF HONORS

Lady,
your body
with its sagged
throne,
your brown-eyed
breasts
in their nested
urn of many kisses,
your dry armpits
too tired
to flow,

lady,
these are no
year-torn
ravages,
no flowerless
stems,

lady,
these are
your medals.

THE SAME LADY

I

I hear April's shudder of gutter lakes,
limbering roots and mud flowing
slick and rich as gravy
in rutted dirt roads, bubbling
along corner lawns walked bare
and seething between the untarred
city slots where the earth leaks
over macadam and cement:
April's ooze and worked-up sweat
making a job of the season.
And I reason that mud
is a sweet old girl's ageless
glands gone wild again for love,
a girl blown lilac-windy and
risen to her sweet numb knees.

II

Fat old lady Spring again.
No sylph-like girl this
bud waddle, green swaddling
and full-grown winds
warning: "Appreciate". We
return to that old juice
hoping to stay loose, stay
loose. But few of us impervious
to May can stand the stake of roses

in the heart, and not go gay,
go adolescent and roundelay,
roundelay. Voom go the pom pom
buds and grasses, slurp goes the sap;
and the pap of the world lifts up, up
to these old humdrum lips; and fe, fo,
fi, fum, this beanstalk giant
tumbles head over shin into
the sweet obesity of Spring.

THE LIGHT AND THE SADNESS

[To Zenna Henderson in gratitude
for her "People"]

And the sadness that is light
blistered and bared her
and she was alone.
                        From the zone
of the sun a voice came like honey
thick and insistent into her
loneliness and its honeycomb.
Bathed in that sweet food she rose
and entered the light till
her skin lay smooth and she was clothed.
And the light that is sadness
burned out in the sun.

GIRL IN A GREEN DRESS

She moves
in a green dress
as a high grass moves
to a rogue wind
and she stands
in a green dress
like clustered stems,
her hair surprised poppies
cresting it all.
And she smiles
in a green dress
silent as scent
and lets
the color work.

HIS WORLD A PIÑATA

[for Dick Banks]

Hyperbole
was what he loved,
taking it in his two hands
and biting in hard.
It's the idiom, the idiom
that makes the man,
he'd cry, pretending to die
right on the sidewalk of a handy world.
Phrase it right
and love's a bird of purple
flying inside out
and the singing right out plain.
But the verb, the verb,
he'd sing,
gently fingering a gentle lady's flesh,
that's the thing to watch
like a bomb
that blows you in
instead of up,
packs it all tight as a piñata
for anyone with a well aimed bat
to break
making it rain birthday and christmas
first, last and every day of this man's made-world.

THE TREES IN HIS HEAD

He has given up
writing in the dust of table tops.
Someone wipes his name away.

Lately

he plants trees in his head
saying *hot ideas need shade.*

Now

something like leaves begins
to grow out of his ears. *April*, he says,
is disappearing around corners.

Yesterday

he stood in the field all afternoon
shadowing the beginnings of a sapling peach,
said, *tomorrow will be green and wind.*
Said, *Son, fruit is a knack.* And
all the way back to the house
cried sap.

This morning he sat

in the backporch sun eating peaches
and all the way down to the road
lay only apple trees.

Someone wipes his name away,

throws peach pits in the trash.

But nights now,
he sleeps in the field.

MR. NO-EARS

You've jammed that dark hat
down
Mr. No-Ears
and put on glasses

but I KNOW YOU.

You were in on the launching
hoping for bombs
in bottles

you watched the only bridge
to the city
burn down.

False mustache and brows
could make your scowl worse,
a bald head better

but still I'D KNOW YOU

in any attic
or cellar

it seems you're always climbing
somewhere

with me just behind
calling for everyone to hear

your name: FAKER, MR. NO-EARS

MOON-MAN NEVER-COMING DOWN

a man with his hat jammed down
running out of town

death-dark under his nails like dirt,
the man life-lovers

run out on a rail, tarred dark,
feathered white

each time
a possible last.

But
I (I) KNOW (know) YOU (you).

A KIND OF LOVE

[for Michael O'Malley]

He wanted to pat
the bellies of pregnant women
and say "well done, well done."
Passing on sidewalks,
hands in pockets, head down,
for the moment that love takes
he loved them,
whispering to each one
like a Father or lover, "good girl, good girl."

THREE FLIGHTS UP IN ROME

Siesta.
The shutters part like cards
(3 flights up)
and she appears
drying her long hair.
Nothing in the street moves
save one cat drunk on heat.
Only (3 flights up)
her brown bare hands
loving her hair dry
move like moles
in and out of the white towel
searching the cave mouth of her head
where darkness is wet, cool
and sings round her head.
Here (3 flights up)
is over the world
where boons
are granted lovers beneath balconies
as tall as this one
and kisses
fall like petals (3 flights down)
into the siesta
where no one
not even now a cat
moves.

He has been washed and locked in
for the night
and the dark outside
is coming down heavy. He could
sleep except for the teacups
chattering upstairs,
except for the darkness
and the coming down
hard. So he sits on the bed
which is his bed and chews
on a peeled sliver of wood
from its headboard. His head
lolls onto one shoulder which moves
as he chews, as the veins in his
temples move. Upstairs talk runs
as normal as water. No one asks
for the little monster of the cellar.
He has been away forever. Later
as the heavy dark lifts
she will come bringing sleep
calling him Sweet Melon
and place his head straight
on the pillow again.

ASYLUM FIRE

"many perished locked in their cells"

The flames danced in
and you curtsied, lady,
and waltzed with your own ashes.
        They said they heard laughter
        and singing in the smoke.

You awoke, sir, to imps of fire
and bargained for your life
with trinkets of cloth and coin.
        They said they heard a calm
        talking as the flames walked in.

They said you were better off, sir, lady;
but coughed softly in their cage of horror.

IVORY TOWER

In a town
where
the academician
wearing rubbers
and carrying
a mushroom umbrella
forgets
that doors
and ladies
are for opening,
the ladies
grow nearsighted,
the hinges rust
and the rain
merely
cooperates.

TRUTH HAS A SINGING

Casals
knew it
in the mornings
when he laid
his music
on the beaches.
Picasso
knew it
in those Spanish
afternoons
when his paint
sang forth
hot tongues.
And Pound
knew it
in the nights
when in that room
within a room
he struck
word after word
like matches
into singing.

PICASSO

He chose
a castle to nest in,

moved in his
exquisite junk,

muraled the old bathrooms
and drank toasts

to the queer ceilings.
His unleashed feelings swam

through castle halls
calling to themselves,

building histories
in his head

while his old thighs
majestically

commenced a climax
in his bed

reminding the startled
castle walls

that history clasped
in the thighs' music

is never dead.

TO RICO LEBRUN AND
ANGER AT BUCHENWALD

Dialed to death
by the cruel simplicity
of numbers, one came back

to tell of crude arabic limbs
and a message sprawled
haphazardly in a pit.

And one came back
to paint a geometry of death
and frighten proper ladies

in their lace collars gliding into
museums, making appalled ohs
into the fine arts air.

One came back to cite humanity
in black and white carnage
of breast and buttocks,

came back to weep
for the human circumstance
and purify his fingers in brutality.

WISHBONE

[for Rico LeBrun who died May 1964]

Now
it's your ribcage
you've yet to paint.

I go to see
that lusty death laid bare, those
bony words hung
like other kinds of corpses.
And I think of you,
of that one time
you chewed my name like a wishbone.

Somewhere your lovely bones bleach
with no one to paint
how they fall,

your wishbone the short half.

A MAN I KNOW

is building
a motorcycle

and has no legs

and we are begged
to listen how the motor runs

and we who listen
are building a sky

and have no wings.

MY HALF OF THE APPLE

You're eating my half of the apple
and I've a right to my own mistakes.
I marked off
where you were to stop eating
but you kept on
and now something in you
is mine. And you're making
my mistakes. If I'm to choose
plums tomorrow, you'll choose pears.
There it is. And the pears
will be green. And there you'll be
sick with my sickness
and I'll be well, out in the sun
making up smiles. So next time
stop. You've your own mistakes to count,
let me keep mine. Not that it's greed,
only a kind of right.

FIGURINE

Imagine me
pure white
with no relief
save merely
intricate engraving.
Then imagine
shadows holding
my design—
script and image.
Imagine me
with white trees
shining up my legs,
my several entrances
filigreed.
Imagine my mouth
an ancient word
spoken white hot.
Imagine my eyes
birds etched in ivory,
my immaculate womb
with a white icon.
Imagine me thus
of pure high white
relieved only
by intimate shadow.

WARNING

This morning the squirrels
make strange noises
and I am afraid.
They make noises I know
they've never made before
or will ever make again.
It's because of the rain
the sky is thinking of
that they make their noise
and because three boys
ran through the yard yelling war,
and at the corner
a bus made a sinister
air-brake hiss. It's because
of this the squirrels make up
their new noise and I know
they mean their warning
to be serious,
afraid because the year
runs late
and the squirrels' quota of time
(along with mine) shrinks faster
when we're not listening.

WHAT GOT AWAY

These wisps of hair in my hand
are enough to tell
who got away.

              It was the way
it always is. You reach
out, catch half the head's hair
in your fist
but not enough to catch the head by.
And it's gone
              Wishes are like that.

This flesh beneath my fingernails?
Well, desires
are like
THAT!

HAPPY BIRTHDAY

I've built you a mountain.

Last Summer, remember
you asked
(humble)
for a hill.

Here it is, mountainous.

Because the rocks
kept appearing
at random
I put them in, then
those trees marching through
dragging that river by its heels.

I had to use everything.

Knowing
you'd never have room
to keep it
I left off the ribbons
and there it is
just as it stood
finished.

Just at the last
when you were nearly due
I brought in birds,
the fish came by themselves

and sometime in between
a bear wandered through.
He's in there somewhere.

I know you
wanted a hill
but you know how I am
when I get started.
There I was in the middle of landslides
and sunsets
thinking how you'd grin

and say
I really wanted a mountain anyway,

so here it is
Happy Birthday.

MIRROR

You there. Someone else.
Some otherness toed for danger,
who are you? Mother you are
not, nor child, nor lady yet as excellent
as your dreaming. Great stranger,
old accuser, last and only hater,
love is your saver. Alien of the clean
glass, we speak mornings and evenings
carefully casual, eternally
the other's leaner. But always
our eyes go strange rather than recognize
a dangerous truth. Our safety
is our separateness.

YOUR HARDS, YOUR EDGES

Rocks, stones, boulders,
I question your hards,
your edges.
Like puzzles
great crevices, smooth
and table ledges
confuse me. Even your
haphazardry troubles me.
Of all enigmas
yours is slyest.
Baked hot and dry
you persevere, slammed wet
and rough you crack shoulders
but grow more stolid. Every
day of the world your solidity
demands nothing, endures;
and if I am sure of anything
it is of you. I may not
understand them
but your hards,
your edges,
enter me.

WHAT I AM ABOUT

am not about
hat they are about.

ily
) mist
I go,
they go,
about something else.

What
I am about
is today
green,
tomorrow
perhaps yellow,
one clean
from the other.

They are about grey
and the quick red flash
of a neon bar
sign. On, off,
from dark
to dark.

But I am not
about what they
are about.
As their sign flashes

I am only
about the moon
coming up,
only about a bending
of trees
and the arms
of Orion.

NOTHING

There is nothing I require.
The roads have been washed
and the island is white. Nothing.
Juice from the fruit trees
waits in the glass, the windows
are honest and open
and crumbs of new-cut bread
cling to my fingers. But knowing
you wish to give me some
intricate thing I listen
to the tears fall in your throat,
tears for all things I do not have.
Still, watching the small dry pink
corners of your eyes
I require nothing.

I TALK OF YOU IN CITIES

I talk of you in cities,
trace your name
on sooted windowpanes.

No one believes me.

I learn to speak of you
casually as I do
of extraordinary flowers
displaced to flower carts.

Still, no one believes me.

More casually, still,
I comment
upon the color of the air
(silently my breast echos
color where your head has been)
and in the afternoons
I speak of how the locusts
strip the sun of logic
(the imprint of your ear
upon my cheek forgives me).

And sometimes, someone believes
nearly all I have not said.

MUCH TOO SANE

Tomorrow I must begin to go mad.
(Much too sane
no one listens anymore).

I've been standing up to all my debts too long.
(Sanity is only an appointment kept
or not, someone met or not).

If you hear me
trying out screams
remember how always on time

I spoke softly, laughed
just loud and long
enough

and when I walk by
with dreams in my arms
heaped high as laundry

don't speak. I'll be going mad.
(Come back later,
I may be back for lunch).

TALES TOLD BY TEXTURES

Take a handful
of crumpled velvet
and let it go

anyone would know
you'd been
there;

and creases of silk
carefully sat on
by behinds

softer than down
they'd tell
where they'd been

too. And the kind
of satin 1920s-women wore
over braless breasts

that told everything
right out quick
like hard nipples.

THE EYES OF THE
PHOTOGRAPHER

We bend to the brook,
beautifully women,
and the water
drips from our hands—
sunlight liquefied.
We have been beautiful
like this forever,
lassoed in photographs of time,
eyes lidded over
drinking time's terrible water,
freezing our beauty
thus. But time ends and
we rise up,
wiping wet hands along our thighs,
looking sudden and truthful
into the frightening eyes
of the photographer.
We cannot lie now
who are no longer
beautiful.

DREAM: THE EYES
DOWN THERE

There was the elevator shaft
and some *thing* half broken at the bottom
half out of light.

No cry came
but wind rumored in the shaft
and two yellow eyes looked up

alive where the light hit,
dead elsewhere.
We, the accused, looked down

from our great height,
looked down along the swaying
cable snakes,

listened for some cry,
some evidence the yellow eyes were live
and sighed when even those lights went out

or walked off where no light lived
and the slippery elevator like a monitor lizard
moved down from the top floor.

HORSES OF STONE

The hazards are there
like stone horses with teeth.
Knowing no horse can bite
like a stone one and none
step higher
           I have gone out
to ride them alone, even
shared saddles with generals.
Bronze horses going green
have leaped between my knees,
tree branches swathed back
to rake my cheek. If you can
believe these old scars,
you can believe the hazards
and the dare. Can believe somewhere
stone horses shy. The trick
is not to be left mounted
on thin air.

RELATIONSHIPS

Going to the store
to buy a melon.
In my two hands it is your head,
gently, gently.
          Going home
the brown paper bag crackles like words,
like names tacked together
or endearments sharp with coinage.
Scrubbing carrots and potatoes of their good dirt
I am smiling
          and from a bowl
black olives look up at me, warm.

5 o'clock in the morning and
               no one here but us.
Here is the usual street
               unusual now because sleep
is the air's caution. No motion but ours.
               There should be milkmen. No one.
Of course birds, always birds even before light
               and we here unusually alert
are a kind of bird, fuzzed by not knowing
               where to go without conversation.
Like a popped toy gun cork a kitchen lightbulb
               goes on. Someone else up.
Broken nobody-else-here-but-us-birds' Spell
               and we think warmly of all the
sprawled or curled people not yet aware
               we are stealing them blind,
stealing this perilous and perfect time. Shhh.

KNEELING BY THE WINDOW

Dark the color of forgotten
money rusts in my purse.

Who comes to spend shall leave receipts.

And pale light
the color of milk
pours from the silk pockets
of my dressing gown.

Having recently risen
sleep stills sounds in my ears
like cups of bees.

Who comes to buy brings awkward money.

Here, kneeling by the window
shadows of birds hurt in my palms.

Having earned these shadows
I give them away

to whoever passes
dark in his pockets,
rust in his mouth.

WHO'S AFRAID

[with thanks to Albee]

I am, I am,
cries the child meaning spiders.
Webs in the wood
that stretch across your face,
dark a place you run out of
brushing off spiderwebs. Like corners.

Afraid?

The rain is there. You start out
expecting to arrive, to find hands.
But the rain starts
and after that someone
always wanting names to things
invents dark
with only the light from owls' eyes to see by.
But we're coming. We're always
coming. Anyone
can live with names.

Afraid of something?

Even in the first tunnel
we're afraid we'll not be born. To make a fist
is learned first
and then
that great knocking

to get out where the stars are. And spiders.
A place to be afraid.
Spiderwebs, rain, all the world's dark places,
we're coming. Fear, the first tooth,
the cry, *I am*,
a sustenance.

Afraid? Of course.

THE QUESTION

Tonight
in the walls
the mice move with circumspection.

The heat in the radiators
makes curious noises
and outside
the owls are dying cold.

Two cats crying head to head
talk to my cat
here indoors.
His fur and ears attend them
as I do,
while in the walls the mice
perform their queer calligraphy.

I turn the lights out
to read these sounds more clearly,
hear the cat's eyes clink,
the owl's click one-at-a-time
and my own primed blood
ticking. The radiators
complain of the dark

like widowed women, the cat
with silk sound
bounds to the windowsill.

To stop the mice
coming out to taste the dark
I snap the lights back on,
and one owl
dying slow and colder than the rest
asks the question
I am careful
never, never
to answer.

FOUND: A SLIP OF ALMOST
WHITE PAPER

If we had lemon juice
this white paper
would be mysterious
but there are no
lemons growing
in our garden.
The ink
remains
invisible,
the message
in tremendous
code
white on white
paper.

Somewhere
someone is keeping
secrets.

Tomorrow
we will plant
lemon trees

just in case.

DARKNESS MAKES US EQUAL

In the dark
time is as blind
as anyone.
Shuffle and stumble
minute by minute,
it could be years
since the light
went out
and this throat
opened. Somewhere
held out
my hands could be timeless.

But I hear
my fingernails
growing even
in the dark.
It could, I could
be blind
in this dark,
but I think
time just turned round
and is heading back
to where
we both came in.
And outside
it may be tomorrow
for all I know.

HEAR

Hear.
I say it
as peacefully
as the sea
secretly says pebbles,
as over the sand
the wind
says mountains.

Hear.
Said as clearly,
as slowly
as roots say the earth,
as the cavern brook
says the running darkness.

Hear.
I say it
as carefully
as my night's imagining
fits its mouth
to the moon's face.

Hear.
Walking up the alleys
of anger, hear,
walking among dreams

your hands fall through.
My saying
will fit its tread
quietly beside yours.
Hear.

PROMISE TO AN UNCONCEIVED CHILD: SOME MONTH, MY SON, SOME YEAR

JANUARY

I name my son Raven.
Too tight with cunning
to be born he burns
his name in monthly
rivers down my thighs.

FEBRUARY

Son, our laugh distills
your sky of lonely weather.
We count upon the abacus
of my ribs how long
the winter river lingers.

MARCH

We learn. Your March voice
rises like a wind beneath
my skin. I hear, son,
but your sky goes thick again,
goes red instead of blue.

APRIL

Monotony has satin walls
you climb and climb again
to end doubled down
like a slug turned round
in sand for exercise.

MAY

We grow to know a more
intimate conversation. We know
your seasons blow by diets
of the moon and why your room
like flowers bursts and builds again.

JUNE

I mark, son, your knocking
in this June of roses, yet
the moon is eaten up once more.
I catch your name in napkins
and our score adds one regret.

JULY

Summer is our common
envelope and contained
by you I entertain a hope
of pollen. Stolen again
like a pigeon you home back.

AUGUST

Son, the locusts storm
this outer afternoon
while you, warm as a kernel
in a comfortable inferno,
await erupting weather.

SEPTEMBER

Yes, the season moves
in colors we have learned
to name, and you fall blameless
down the moon like a leaf
caught by the air's habit.

OCTOBER

To you, intricate as mist,
smoke must also be a puzzle.
In belly braille I instruct your senses
so you can understand why smoke
auctions off October.

NOVEMBER

Ice begins, but I can never
teach you cold. I keep
you folded in renewing
warmth. Cold is solid
and you approach a liquid.

DECEMBER

Raven, this festive air
enhances our communication.
My body wraps you like a gift.
I tell you the story of
another's long born son . . .

I name my son Raven.
Stalking birth on some
peculiar pivot he burns
his name in monthly
rivers down my thighs.

TWO REASONS FOR
THE PHANTOM CHILD

I

I am house, room, box,
am bottle, cup, thimble
from which
nimble as water
my child goes
fallible as a gem breaking.
Hands he has not grown
splay on my womb-wall,
feet he does not own
push out his plug.
He is my regular
hug, wish, hope, whim,
and with him I am spilled again,
and again for him
am filled
as a house, room, box,
as a bottle, cup, thimble.

II

Little thigh of my thigh,
you've slipped off again
and why
is an old memory.
Sorrier than ever
you forgive me,

arm of my arm, beginning
back with no more alarm
than a possible ache. Cheek
of my cheek, you disarm me
with your probable smile,
dissolve me, wrist of my wrist,
with your possible pulse.
I remember you or else
forget myself, body of my body,
self of myself.

A POEM OF AND

And the light
made it morning
and the birds
and the sounds
peculiar to it
made it morning.
And because
it was another
morning I made
peace with it
as one does,
with rituals
of water
and dropped
clothing. And
because of the peace
it was easier
to say *thank you*
when no one asked
because *thank you*
tasted as sharp
and clean
as mint leaves.
And because
this was the right way
to say a morning
into itself

in an entirely
personal manner
the whole day
slid down
like a silk slip
over talc'd skin,
and to say *please*
out of a blue sky
was as easy
as whistling
on grass blades.
And because
it got dark
and night
was to give to,
you're welcome
became the last
whisper before
sleep.